£8.50

Gallery Books
Editor Peter Fallon
SCAPEGOAT

Alan Gillis

SCAPEGOAT

Gallery Books

Scapegoat
is first published
simultaneously in paperback
and in a clothbound edition
on 1 October 2014.

The Gallery Press
Loughcrew
Oldcastle
County Meath
Ireland

www.gallerypress.com

*All rights reserved. For permission
to reprint or broadcast these poems,
write to The Gallery Press.*

© Alan Gillis 2014

ISBN 978 1 85235 609 5 *paperback*
        978 1 85235 610 1 *clothbound*

A CIP catalogue record for this book
is available from the British Library.

Scapegoat receives financial assistance
from the Arts Council.

Contents

Zeitgeist *page* 11
Instagrammatic 13
The Hourglass 16
Lunch Break on a Bright Day 18
Spring 22
The Allegory of Spring 23
August in Edinburgh 27
No. 8 28
The Same Again 35
Aubade 37
The Estate 39
Bulletin from The Daily Mail 41
21 Poinsettia Avenue 42
Somewhere Near the Dockyards 44
Nostalgia 47
40 48
Les Creux de l'Esprit 49
The Return 50
The Lounge 51
Before What Will Come After 52
The Field 54
A Further Definition of Memory 56
Green Odes 61
Scapegoat 62
The Wake 67
Morning 69
The Scattering 70
The Sweeping After 71
River Mouth 74
One Summer Morning 76
The Rose Beds 77
Night Song for Rosie 81
The Sweeping 82

Acknowledgements 87

'The harvest is past, the summer is ended, and we are not saved.'
— Jeremiah, 8:20

Zeitgeist

I look for you behind retail parks,
ghost-lit showrooms, in dark
scrubland where plastics flutter on coils
of barbed wire; where, through mean soil
strewn with pipes, cartons, slugged condoms,
streams a steep-edged brook. Drawn
to its burble and splurge
I slip on the verge, fall and splunge
stretching for the banks, reeds, not catching hold
of anything sound, my hands ice-cube cold.
And past megastores, waste yards, the suburbs' borders,
carried along on colourless waters
ever gushing on, with no smile, no frown,
I call you down, I call you down.

❖

City limits are fine but I spend most
days hemmed in, meshed and lost
up a tower — in front of a screen,
black plastic keyboard, black plastic machine
on a laminate desk — where the windows
don't open much in case I throw
myself out. Dust gathers on the phone,
empty plant pots. I am alone
much of the time to the extent
that a vague itch of harassment
prickles my contact with people.
And vacuumed through the non-soul
of blank matter, with no smile, no frown,
I call you down, I call you down.

❖

Outside on shopped streets swarm mothers,
alpha males, screenagers, old, young, lovers,
the homeless, the bewildered, ill, unique,
the beautiful with their self-as-boutique —
so many, thronged into one body,
surrounding me, squishing, cumbering me
with sucken hair and grey breath,
a cracked open swallowing mouth.
And looking through a million eyes,
slouching upon a million thighs
compelled by the shackles
of meat-headed instinct to slowly circle
around and around, with no smile, no frown,
I call you down, I call you down.

❖

Inside the machine or, at least, on the screen
I discover everything that has been,
will be, or might never be has a place.
You can search for God, your name, any face
and reconfigure. You can hurt someone
and they won't know it was you. There's a room
for all things, the wall of each room an exit
to all that's possible, all interconnected
with, as they say, no edge and no centre.
I press enter and enter and enter,
not knowing where to go, what I might find
in this flat expanding surveillant mind,
weightless, free floating, with no smile, no frown,
I commune. Then the machine powers down.

Instagrammatic

The camera went snap and the moment
was captured. It was a glorious day.
But when I picked up the photograph
weeks later the image was skew-whiff,
like a cover version of the scene
I remembered. The sky, I'm sure,

was picture-book azure, not pasty duck-
egg and mackerel. The trees were *Vogue*
magazine green but, in our photo, dull
as a self-printed Plymouth Argyle fanzine.
And we were not like ourselves. Life-
sized cardboard cut-outs of Mario and Luigi

in a shop window Nintendo display
look more true to life. It was as if look-
alike actors had taken our place
and I imagined a set-up where we pay
stand-ins to replicate scenes of our life
while we work overtime in grey rooms

to pay them. I wondered, what chance
have words, if even in a photograph
from a Sony Cyber-Shot DSC-RX 100
the living moment is caged, held off-stage?
All that we might see or say is half-wrong.
We approximate one another. Then we're gone.

And so, though I've been with you now
for donkey's years, if I were to speak of how
I want to lick your eyebrows, but don't dare risk it,
or say your ears are biscuits,
your teeth scream,
your lips are the crystal violet contours of a recurring dream,

your hair cries,
your nipples are eyes,
your tongue is a lizard,
your passing youth is melting lard,
and when you tilt your head at nothing much to surprise
   me with a grin
I'm a forest of fir trees shoogled in the wind,

and your sense of humour is a ferret,
your nose is a white-sided jackrabbit,
the sweat on the curve of your neck is the dew on a tulip's calyx,
your irises are the aurora borealis
(and if these are windows to your soul, then you're a
   chameleonic shimmering megaton
of colliding electric particles blown by the sun),

and your stomach is a sand dune,
your dress is a lambent field of wheat blown gently in June,
your legs are identical twins,
your chin is a dove or, at least, you have a bar of Dove soap
   for a chin,
and when I reach for you I press against a windowpane,
scattered, dripping, splattered drops of shivered rain,

and your heart is an ocean liner that has sunk,
your fingers are a crack team of commandos, but your toes
   are drunk,
your laughter is a round of applause,
your bank balance is that scene where Robert Shaw gets eaten
   in *Jaws*,
and I'm sorry I'm a banjaxed replica backstreet device,
all wind and spleen, no fire nor ice,

and your backside is a birthday cake,
your memories are a rainbow cloud of dragonflies above
   a darkening lake,
your frown is a gun,
your happiness is summer grass bleaching in the sun,
and your remaining days are shorebirds swooping through an
   almond-streaked sky over the vast Atlantic's oncoming night,
then remember, my love, I might not be half-right.

The Hourglass

Time falls like rain
in the hourglass I keep turning over,
carried from the cupboard to your gingham-
covered deal table, trying to pother
the grains in your swept kitchen
on my first sleepover
at yours. You ask: 'One half empties, the other
fills. Now which half is happier?'

Both ends look dead by the end.
The hourglass shows how time gathers
but only lives through the movement of the sands.
Time suffocates the sphere it enters,
voids what it leaves behind.
Through a window the shadows of alders
jig across the room as you spool your reel,
then roll in tinfoil two big tuna rolls.

Up before dawn so we can have lines in
the river for sunrise, the blanket
bog's surface glistens like fish skin
breathing in the moonlight.
I have read in *The Book of Great
Facts* that bogs don't grow, they accumulate
and I can believe it in my bobble hat,
borrowed twelve-eye boots and puffed jacket.

'Keep your eyes on your feet,'
you say, 'this'll be the making of ye.'
Then a sudden sheep
gives me the skites and I slip on the scree
of the hill as it bleats
and shrieks, niddle-noddles its straggly
backside up the hillside
like a black-shawled old woman shaking her head.

Reaching higher ground I turn to look
back on the sweep of heather and sedge
quilting the slopes and sheughs
before we pass the high ridge
and traipse downhill to bait our hooks.
Lines ready at the slosh of the river edge,
you turn to me in the sough of daybreak:
'Remember, take and give, give and take.'

Now time has spilled its darkness over you
I could say I'm back on those pitch
black fens once again, unable to
tell a hawthorn bush from a furzy ditch,
sludging to reach the stead of you
somewhere over the ridge
among shadows, sundews and fronds,
casting in the glent of the riverbend.

But I only stayed with you that one time
because of your drinking. Under a fleering moon
in a black-shawled night sky I dream
breathing sphagnum, moorgrass and broom
enter my body, like the taste of brine.
A cold shiver. How the rain and wide-roamed
dead, rivers and wilds, give and take,
hollow as they accumulate.

Lunch Break on a Bright Day

If you lie on your back,
buck naked within your clothes,
under a beech or ash
tree's secluded grove

of park grass, letting
time pass with bird
nests above you
and a sound-quilt of bird

song about you,
as if in an alcove
looking up at a sun-spritzed
stained glass window,

watching the city's smoke
billow and waft
in delicate mallow puffs,
creamed meringue rafts

floating in the blue
lagoon sky,
you might come to suspect
the concourse between your eye

and brain,
for just like those old tubed
kaleidoscope toys you put
to your eye and turned

so everything went
Lucy in the Sky,
the sunlight wheels
and turns as you lie

within the umbra
of the tree
while the rinsing breeze
ripples the leaves

and sashaying twig-tips
with a shush
to the ear,
and each swish

of that green hair sprays the air
with glittered drops of bright
molten flushing amber,
lemon beads of light

in a river of glints,
a gush of glimmer-flow,
so you understand
the proposition *there is no*

fixed position
is now the only
fixed position,
for you can't take in this one tree,

the bark-brown
rutty dark of its bole,
its thick arms
upholding aureoles,

flavescent weavings,
branches sprouting
out of branches,
sprigs and spangs spouting

into a four thousand-
fingered trick of light,
pearl and honey
twinkling through slight

chinks between leaves,
glancing eyes through fronds,
micro-tints of ruby,
wet gleams of blonde

and bottle green,
leaf-tips like the lime
in a sharp tequila
and fizzed lime

soda sparkled with ice
trickling through a thin
multi-leaved
fluent-edged flim

of illuminated green
and aquamarine,
emerald, acid green,
avocado and margarine

until your head dances off
leaving you with luminance
in a haze of movement,
an overload of sense

and absence of reason
with which to rise
unsteady to your feet,
rub your twizzled eyes

and return to the city's
vast and hurried goad
of information flows,
firewalls, barcodes,

streets that give no pleasure
today when you walk, as you must,
back to work through the rot
and the rust and the ashes and the dust.

Spring

You might have butterflies
for no reason, all antsy
as if in anticipation
of the leaves' first look-and-see-me.

You might crack your nut trying to take in
the what of it, its here and this
while it lifts its skirts to brush by you,
fleeting past with one light kiss.

Bare-knuckled sycamores start wearing green.
Cherry blossom froths and pirouettes
in a brook, trickling past these streets
and estates, sloshing beneath tarmac,

visible here, underground there, everywhere
guzzling as the narrow-banked brook
rushes past scraggy reeds and weed tufts,
cacked plastics, sewer scurf, beer-can stooks,

streaming along in the green-glinted leaf-swish
and ripple of a petal-scented zing,
and with it flows all that we know of the here-
it-comes and there-it-goes of everything.

The Allegory of Spring

What pleasures we might find
    pass on.
Nothing to be done. Like air
    they are not long

to be held. Fast shadows darken
    fresh grass
and most of what we know
    grows bored

inside us. Like the sadness
    of money.
Like the measure of a median life,
    a McLife

like this one, rising to fall, falling
    to rise.
Yet here comes everyone —
    one by one

they peep their heads,
    creep out
from the dark to bud and spume
    like wild

fire into a teeming forest. There is
    something
mental about birth. You couldn't
    make it up:

the fury in seeds. Death not out-
    done. Death out-
doing us, our ceremonies,
    reaching

for the intangible, the way
    it drifts
like mist from a scalded
    teapot,

the tint of irises we never
    notice
in the vase, in the corner
    of the room,

until they're dying. Or that scent
    of moss
in the cover of the wood, creeping
    thistle,

greenfinches trilling in the brake
    as if for us
on that walk I never wanted to take,
    then dreamed

about for nineteen years. Oh lay
    me low.
Convolvulus and daffodils, the glissade
    of beech leaves.

Lay me down in a shaded glade, though I
    could count
the woods I've walked through in the past
    nineteen years

on one hand and in that time
    I must have
been to Tesco near four thousand times
    taking four times

a week as a likely average. The soft prickle
   of twayblade.
Fingers in the soil. Grass in the mouth.
   Soft docken

leaves on buttercup-stained skin.
   What I like
best are garden centres, the calm trickle
   of their water

features, customers reverential
   in the ambience
of high ferns and pot plants. If we could rip
   the veil of habit,

witness the world truly, we would
   throw up.
And I hear their low moan, a woman
   and man

fucking in a supermarket
   toilet
because they've had it up to here. Hands on
   her buttocks,

he tries to look the way he thinks
   he should
look, though his back hurts. Foxglove
   and may bells,

hair on willowherb, nipples, genitals,
   cellophane.
He hopes she's feeling what she should
   be feeling.

She feels the muffled sorrow
    and need
in the breath of pleasure. When he comes
    she hugs him

but can't wrap herself around all
    this plenty.
Done, they close their eyes and cradle
    themselves

in that blindness. Then, as we all do,
    hoping
for the best, they creep through the door
    one by one.

August in Edinburgh

Not a cloud in the sky and it's raining.
It's the brusqueness of things,
and the drag of things, that hurts.
The most beautiful woman in the world
is in Edinburgh, at the festival.
She looks me in the eye and says please
move I'm trying to look at the artworks.

My doctor says the heart works
but don't push it. I hear music,
long familiar songs, everywhere I go.
Pain is in the mind, someone tells Leonardo
DiCaprio in *Shutter Island*. Everyone
is rushing but the crowd moves slow.
Leonardo can't get his head around it.

A man in costume shouts we've sold out here,
holding his hat out for money and rain.
The mind is an island and everyone
is beautiful, looking for something new
again. But nothing connects, and it's cold.
My son sticks my phone charger in his ear
and says I've got an electric brain.

I've been streaming old LPs I never thought
I'd hear again, never thinking the old songs
would not work, trying not to work the brain,
trying not to rise to the bait when that long
familiar voice rises from the damp and dismal
crowd, once again, to say hey, if we all think
hard enough, maybe we can stop this rain.

No. 8

I'm waiting for a bus.

❖

There's a man at the bus stop.

❖

I count the change
in my hand three times
in the space of
twenty-seven seconds.

❖

The man at the bus stop
does not acknowledge me.

❖

Neither of us stands still
as if we both need to go
to the toilet.

❖

I'll go nuts if the bus doesn't

❖

Ah here it comes, like a big post box.

❖

I count my change
again and watch to see if the man
will make some sort of signal
to stop the bus
but he's playing it cool
leaving me uncertain
as to whether I should
also play it cool or signal
when the bus indicates to pull
over of its own accord,
which is a relief.

❖

The driver looks like someone
has just wiped his face
with a monkfish.

❖

The bus carriage is how I imagine
a train carriage might be
on a night train to Volgograd.
There is a smell of underwear.

❖

Everyone looks like
they're in an art installation
where the central concept is
they're completely normal.
They don't acknowledge me
with, as it were, studiousness.
I get a seat on my own.

❖

Yes!

❖

I wonder if anyone on the bus
is focusing
on a man or on a woman
and is imagining that
that man or woman is thinking
about getting their hole
or about when they last had their hole.

❖

Then I worry someone might be
wondering the same about me
and I resent the intrusiveness
and begin to wish
I wasn't on the bus
and I read a newspaper
left on the seat next to me
to take my mind off things.

❖

The bus chugs its way
along the inner city road,
a sluggish river,
shoals of people on the pavements,
all of them looking mad
and beautiful,
some touching one another
most not, my God

how can it be
this void of substance?

❖

I mean the newspaper.

❖

The woman in front
of me has texted
dont spend ur money!!!
really fast

❖

I should have brought a book,
something with rhythm
and point.
Those priceless devices.
Point and rhythm.
One morning you come down
the stairs and they're gone.
A note on the table.
You recognize them in others,
from time to time,
in the street.

❖

Busaroo. Busaroo. Bus-a-doodle-doodle-doo.

❖

Extremely expensive and desirable
large cars of immaculate design
and awesome engineering pass by
like concrete signifiers
of the self-as-sexual-fantasy
of their drivers
who thereby assert their victory
in the perpetual
battle of the body and soul
against the void
while effectively pissing
on the 22,000 children
in the world who die
from preventable poverty daily.

❖

Does one have depths?
To get to them, I'm sure,
one might board a bus.

❖

There's the man
from the bus stop
getting off the bus
and walking away,
his jacket slung
over his shoulder
for it is quite close,
walking into the crowd
like he doesn't care;
but I think this is to mask
deep cares
as he enters the anonymous

heart of the bruised city
swallowed whole
by the beautiful shoal
of his mad
questing unknown
brothers and sisters.

❖

Alone and crowded
going in the usual direction
slowly this is the essence
I must acknowledge
of my being.

❖

A woman has some bother
getting on the bus
not having the right change
saying she didn't know the fare
had changed
as if these days you could not be aware
that everything changes
except for the principle
that everything changes.

❖

So much mystery between us
disguised as indifference.

❖

Such proximity
disguised as distance.

❖

Aloof and dependent
the antechamber of the soul
could not be solitary and static
although, I'm sure,
it might feel solitary and static.

❖

We're all in this together.

❖

The sunlight
as the bus comes
onto North Bridge
gleams glint-bright
scintillating architecture.
Sometimes I feel like a feather
swept this-a-way lifting
that-a-way through the heavens
of my time and place here
on earth
while nonetheless
sitting on a bus.

The Same Again

I board my evening bus for the dark hall
and house that pull me in, take
me from the day. Cornered by painted walls
I spill red wine, with shaken hands, stab a steak.

Outside the young and police vans bawl.
A silent cat, whiskers caked,
licks a furred corpse between its paws.
Shagged dogs pillage cowped street bins.

Foxes roam, their eyes patched moons,
while in my plummet of pillow and linen
images sprout, strew and mushroom.
I leach, ooze and swirl in burns,

runnels, sluiced through drain-
pipes and culverts where I swill
underground with the bilge, draff and grain
clogged in the throat of this town while

again and again and again and again
strange-tongued night-shifters board
their night bus, from Olangapo, Malenville,
to make their way to sullen offices and wards.

Rings around her eyes, bitten by the chill,
a cleaner from Lodz swears at the stench
of the hotel bar's blocked toilet,
then plunges rubber gloves into the squelch.

And her fingers probe through me, squidge
through my dregs, my eddies and driblets
cupped and coming together in the scrunch
of her hands like eggs into an omelette

that the wealth-holed and mouth-
shaped city beholds, then swallows back
into the night of itself,
waiting to break.

Aubade

The ambience of night creeps and swirls
in a haze, sifts and curls

in your ear as you drift through quiet
darkness, when I recognize it,

its qualming tones, for what it is
and it holds me pinned in its icy hizz,

its nauseous waves of arrhythmia;
then I wake up in a clapped-out Kia

Picanto or Škoda in a car park,
litter rasping sinister through the dark,

and I fly for a nearby wood of yews
tweeting where are you, I've been true

and how I miss the brightness,
wild strawberries, watercress,

for here grow only yew berries and yew
needles and I'm failing to

follow the thread as I'm thrown
by winds over feeming city zones,

valleys of silt, razor mountains
as if the earth had eaten the heavens,

gnawed to bone all I had known
and I flap over dry reservoirs, blown

electrical grids, ash-covered campuses,
back to the yews, dark as molasses,

bristling in the wind like the pelt
of something surviving while rain welts

my skin, clouds expectorate
and I hear the waves crunch and grate

a song of ice and salt darkness coming through —
if you wake up tomorrow it cannot be you.

The Estate

Blotches on walls and much dog
shit on pavements, hedges full of crisp bags,
chip bags and cans,
an eye at every window for the postman,
anyone at all, anything coming
or going, or unbecoming.

❖

Well I couldn't stop cringing,
stuffing his face
with Monster Munch, like totally impinging
on my personal space,
and when I said so he was like look here missus
this here's a public bus.

❖

An old fridge in the garden,
a boy showing his hard-on,
tracksuit bottoms pulled tight,
saying her tits were satellite
dishes, saying she burnt her ears on his thighs
with sullen eyes, sullen eyes, sullen eyes.

❖

A flutter in the bookies and a fiver to put
before the wife. No football boots or
fresh fruit or computer
for the kids. No pay-per-view.
No suit
for a funeral, an interview.

❖

Text sex, porno moans
in school corridors,
love rats on the floor
filming vajazzles on their phones.
Kylie's a dog. Tracey's a whore.
Ben has Simone groaning for his ringtone.

❖

You queue and queue
for the intimidation of a too-
tidy desk, swanky office gear,
the bulletproof screen crystal clear.
Hello I'm here to kill you,
please sign here, here and here.

❖

Don't be sayin but e thinks e's humungous.
On tha Viagra an then some, ah'm tellin ya.
But sweaty balls. Fer Christmas e gave us
knickers that cut right inta
ma hole, an gave is fiancée Nigella
fuckin Lawson. Eh? Wha? Nah, she's gorgeous.

❖

Sigourney was down to her knickers and vest,
the alien about to spring, when the fucking *doorbell* rings.
No the repo, but the Green Party canvassing.
I said I like your manifesto, put it to the test.
Oh go for a while with no cash flow no tobacco no quid pro quo
no Giro no logo no demo no lotto no blow no go no go no go
   no no no.

Bulletin from The Daily Mail

You must have seen those Rent Street potheads,
their skin all sweating processed chicken meat:
knives taped to their thighs, blood-red dots for eyes,
stolen shoes like rocketblasters on their feet?

As sure as rainfall, they're at the entrance to the mall,
tattooed necks livid with love bites.
Hooked to mobile phones, they know your way home
and they wait for you in alleyways at night.

They spit on the bus, their fingers are warty,
they set fire to schools, sniff WD40,
they climb any fence, they climb any roof,
they jump on your bonnet and smash your sunroof,

they'll squeeze through your window and creep up your stairs,
they'll leave your comb crawling with their pubic hairs,
they'll crowbar your gold teeth right out of your head,
they excrete on the street, and they don't go to bed.

21 Poinsettia Avenue

Oh my God have you seen Agnes McGarrigan's new hairdo?
When I saw her out with her shih-tzu,
her make-up, her clothes, her whole style
was different. And she carried the strangest smile.
Then again, when she put on *The Best Exotic Marigold Hotel*,
  when we were last round for tea,
she stared so *intently* at Bill Nighy she near spilled the semi-
  skimmed over Doreen McLaverty
and I saw *Fifty Shades of Grey* and Xbox *Zumba Fitness*
on her shelf beside the box sets of *Silent Witness*
and there's no doubt the heels have been getting higher on her
  shoes
and the week before, when that young Piotr called in for his
  brew —
aye, nice big fella, on the Massey Ferguson Tractor —
she was giddy as a contestant on *X Factor*,
Doreen says, as God is her witness, getting on like a devil,
  acting suggestive,
licking the edge of a chocolate digestive.
You'd think she'd be content with a green and crème E-class
  Mercedes Benz,
five bedroom farmhouse, me and Doreen for friends,
an annual two-week all-inclusive in Thessaly
(always the same place, the staff so lovely, like friends really).
But wait, a customer's come through on webcam
so I'm putting you on hold for a minute. OK, Nan?
Oh! *Hi there sexy!* You wanna *play* with me?
You wanna play with my *pussy*?
Oh, you naughty man! You wanna put it *here*?
Let me get the camera closer. You see it clear?
What if I rub it, mmnnn? Ooohhhh that's right.
Uh-huh. Call you Trevor? Oh Trevor, it's so tight.
You're big Trevor! Ooohhhh . . . Trevor? . . . You there, Nan?
Aye, a quickie. Still, it's silver in the hand.

Nah, it's just when they call they're already most-ways there but like I was saying, you really need to see Agnes McGarrigan's hair!

Somewhere Near the Dockyards

And then I come from out the slipways
and tangled flyovers,
multi-lane traffic flowing all-ways,
to high slum buildings near toppled over.

Smoker's-finger yellow, burnt orange,
bloomed boxer's-eye:
the buildings are kippered, a curtain of fish
hung from the absent rafters of the sky.

I enter the mouth of one,
meat and piss in the air,
and climb the teeth of its stairs,
its bannister curling around my backbone.

Jittered from nose-tip to toes
my eyes are frazzled as I come
to a high ceiling room lit by a lunatic sun
imprisoned behind wire-grilled windows.

Like the workings of a mind made visible
dust specks spiral
in clusters and clouds to sift
through slow air in an aimless, limitless drift.

In the middle of the room a brisk
foreman in overalls with oil-slicked hair
bends over blueprints on a desk
making adjustments with compass and square.

A civil servant looks on
taking photos on his smartphone.
They both frown. And though
I can't see I can feel in my bones

they're looking down on blueprints of me.
I can't move nor speak nor
make a dent in the world whatsoever.
They don't notice me

at all, but roll up the prints and suddenly
I'm like bungee
jumping, harnessed to a cord that unwinds
from the absent rafters of my mind.

And then I come to a low razzled
building, the logo
of its neon sign a go-go
girl kicking her heels in a cocktail glass

singing 'I Feel Love' while a man
with oil-slicked hair in military uniform
lunges at the air with a knife and hollers
as I run from his eyes of burning dollars

and it's pissing down rain
and a woman with orange hair beckons
me into her room of bleach and incense,
lily tattoos all over her, but I abstain

to enter a quiet room instead,
sparse but neat,
its single light a lantern
upon a desk with a pile of paper sheets

over which I bend my head
to study and cram
for decades, looking for the pattern.
And then I come to an open span

of green grass, a public park flushed
with oleander, a white rush
of feathered clouds floating through
brilliant birdsong blue.

They don't notice me at all,
parents doting over prams,
dogs wagging through daffodils,
children with whim-whams,

mayflies zigzagged over may bells,
lovers with glossed mouths snogging,
and I think what the hell what the hell,
the civil servant on his phone nodding.

Nostalgia

I too lived somewhere. Life had shape
I dream of now: journals and Schweppes,
candles stubbed in empty bottles of wine,
a painted plank on two wrapped bricks lined

with midnight blue vials of liniment
and balms for her pulverulent
arm skin, mornings spent in the afternoons
reading *L'Imitation de Notre-Dame la Lune*.

I wonder what she thinks of the latest
poetry, she was so earnest —
it was always more than just text for her —
the faux-whimsy of its non sequiturs.

I think she's in retail now
but the surprise is there's no surprise — how
imperceptibly we perceive it's too late
to be free, get a grip, give life shape.

40

Coming up to forty, life's a load
of balls — a straight and featureless road
of rain patter, wiper swish, tyre slosh, landscape blur;
a diesel engine's sinister, somnolent purr.

You come to at the wheel
to realize you're in fifth gear and feel
freaked because you don't know for how long you were
spaced, like you weren't even there,
just a console and windscreen,
a dark stain snaking through the green.

Each time you hit a straight the rim
of the moon looms like a bug-eyed loony bin
in the middle of nowhere, not knowing where
you're going and more than halfway there.

Les Creux de l'Esprit

The mind is like a Wednesday morning
on a bus to work when exhaust fumes cling
the air, past pedestrians with thin screens
for faces, drivers holding back a scream
in cars at loggerheads with the traffic
flow, shaking off the phantasmagoric
night with cappuccino, Red Bull, ginseng,
anxious for what the day might bring.

And Wednesday mornings are not unlike
a wedding — everyone in fright
of not being on time, looking their best;
all they are and hope to be expressed
in their ensemble; gathered in rows
to bless continuance, the crimson rose
bouquets' radiance. But the bride is late
so they fidget with silence, and wait.

The groom shifts in his shoes
smiling. From straight-backed pews
heads crane to peer down the aisle
through an atrium that frames miles
of wide-eyed blue, undulations of green
fields and barley fields, the brook's winding vein
through an oak's shadow — the cadence
of its leaves rumouring the silence.

The Return

The next time I went home
I vowed truly to go home: one young one
head deep in the bloops and beeps of a phone

game, the other on a karaoke
microphone, her smile like piano
music with the wife hovering low-key

at the kitchen door, a grin on her mush,
saucepans frizzling. Before we settled down to it
I pulled the curtains against the brattle and whoosh

of the windows from the evening wind's gusts.
Later, the house quiet, I let
hot suds, once everything gleamed, suck and slush,

gargle into the hollow of the drain.
And in the dark hallway a hazy form
in the mirror asked, who are you again?

The Lounge

I go back to the living
room once everyone is asleep.
On the sofa's scuffed surface amid deep
piles of plastic tat, scraps of toys lying
across the old carpet's stained green,
dust on the blank television, I dream.

Silently I pass through the door
and find him lying there — that man
whose eyes I must gouge to holes
through the bottomless smoke-green floor,
my bone house in my hands, if I am
to enter the world of souls.

Before What Will Come After

Morning, when it comes, might ease the burden
the way McCandless, when I flipped him the bird in
1984 and he went buck mad altogether,
hunting me down like spleen-clouded weather
through the estate, up winding hill-lanes
into Killynether — hounding till we came

to thorn scrub where I got tangled,
snagged and haw-stained in bramble
as he viced me in a headlock, towed
me through green wood to an ash by the road,
the bracken in my ear an itching noise —
rubbed moss in my face, then yanked off my corduroys.

Morning, when it comes, might well stuff a thumb
in this seep of night-tremors, for what will come
could surely not outweigh the heavy night's
burden of waiting for it. Thinking back on it,
bar the cuts and bruises, it was a geg
the way McCandless hung my breeks, as if with pegs

on a line, on one of the ash branches
hung over the road, then fell on his haunches
and broke his hole laughing. Not that it felt
funny right then, I suppose: nettle welts,
aching arms, tree spleets poking at my thighs,
snatters streaming from nose and eyes.

Morning, when it comes, might snigger
the way Shonagh O'Dowd raised her finger
to McCandless, then split her smackers
at the sight of me in my undercrackers
dangled over the road, clinging to the tree,
as she drove past in her Ma's Mitsubishi.

I can still feel my raw hands lose grip
of the shaking branch, the breeze-trembled tips
of the leaves. I'm still trying to grapple
with the wood, my spinning head unable
to take in the slopes of overripe whin,
deep fields, blue lough, curved roads, all in a spin:

Shonagh O'Dowd a big-bellied teenage bride;
McCandless inside, then outside, then inside,
then scot-free altogether, to do harm
here and there, guns in McGilligan's farm
somewhere, wrapped deep in turnip fields;
her leaf-green eyes, all spinning like a flywheel.

My body aches, my ears buzzed with furze, stunk
by the night, sinking through the ash's trunk.
Her lying back in the ferns and harebells.
Him teaching me to smoke by the quarry's walls.
Laughter like bird noise, through the screeching leaves,
laughter in the night, in the pillow sleeves.

Morning, when it comes, will be welcome
as McCandless was when he helped me down
from the ash, grabbed my slacks, called me a tit
while I hoicked them back up on me by the pockets,
my ears huzzing, hiding my shaking hands
as we talked mushrooms, home games, bands,

the apple-flesh of Shonagh O'Dowd's thighs;
and I came alive in the sharpness of his eyes,
darting, ready to target what they could,
making our way back through that green wood
in lines straight as the woodcock's flight.
Morning may come, but this will be a long night.

The Field

This lane can't help but lead
onto that lane I followed
when I was nine, stretched to green
fields from my aunt's farm
along the hedgeway that gives,
through a gap, to a blackthorn-guarded glade

where my catty older cousin says he'll drop me
from the roof of the cow barn onto the cows
if I don't follow the rules and chant
'Rise wormwood eyes' thirty-three times
with eyes shut so the dead can crawl
from the ground where they were murdered.

Sunlight streaks through the copse,
dribbles over honeysuckle
as a cabbage white flickers, a nervous
hand over black sloes; and under bridal-
white fluttering leaves I wheeze
'Rise wood dies' and half-open my eyes.

From the axe wound of a fungal
tree-stump they creep with bramble
fingers, bedstraw genitals, leaking hedge-
parsley. Light melts through their gaped
flowers, their tongues of ret flax.
My hidden cousin wets his kecks.

My mother played in those feeding
grounds as a child before upping sticks
for the city. Staying at the house
of her birth for the holidays, my aunt
had proposed a picnic. And I would
follow the lane, enter the green field,

join those women in the meadow clover
and columbine, rings on their fingers
like marigolds, breaking fresh bread
but I shrink in the glade, waiting to be ravelled
with furze-brake and thorn-roots and to twist
for the rest of my days in this wake of the dead.

A Further Definition of Memory

I had a mate called Snot
who had a sister called Chris
and their Da was shot
on 1st September 1986
(all names and dates have been altered).
Long ago, I'm sure, I forgot
the details, and I don't consciously reminisce,
but dream and dream again of that summer.

There were seven girls on our estate
and to follow the thread
of their chatter was to be reduced to a state
by seven bobbing heads
as they nattered — perched on low
walls or behind hedgerows
in McGarrigan's fields — headspun
and swept up in their twittered, chittered song.

Chris was always in the middle
with ribbon-braided hair and short
primrose-print skirt, and when she sat
on walls the back of her snow-
bright thighs turned red and ridged as a griddle.
Our mate Greener, out of earshot
of Snot, said he wanted to run his fingers
along those soft tracks, to see where they go.

We would go beyond the barley fields
at the edge of town, through narrow
borage-strewn paths edged with hedge nettle,
the shadows of hazels — a thin brook's wheeze
in the ear, pylons humming, cold winds
streamed through sunlight — to while away
afternoons in sweet vernal-grass and play
do or dare, spin the bottle, shoot the breeze.

Greener said he'd ride
anyone, any game wee
girl, only — get this — he wanted to have sex
on the computer. Like, with her backside
on the keyboard kind of thing. Then Snot
said, well, she'll sure need to be wee
for you've only got
a Spectrum ZX.

Our town was a steaming green-brown
turd of a place with a Chinese, chippies,
graffiti, hairdressers, offies, closed-down
offices, bookies, more graffiti,
pool hall, nine pubs and video
library with posters of Chuck Norris videos.
On fair nights the seven girls perched in the town
square like birds. Twitching. Looking around.

But telephone wires crackled overhead and hummed
with humdrum mm-hmns,
uh-huhs, awkward silences, paroxysms
of verbal violence, surveillance,
the coded whispers and cootchie-coos
of the horny arranging rendezvous,
apologies, demands, self-reflections,
vernaculars of throat-cracked wide affection.

First day back at school and Mr Cree had Greener
in front of class looking
in the mirror and repeating
I am stupid, I am nothing.
Sure beats the cane said Greener
with a big beamed smile afterwards,
for Chris had patted his palpitating
chest and said pay no mind, they're only words.

That was the first of September,
I remember, and Chris and Snot's Da
was on night shift and their Ma
went out to Monday Night Maxi-Bingo
so Chris already had two or three fingers
of her Da's vodka in her Um Bongo
by the time I arrived with Greener
who'd nicked cans of warm Smithwicks.

We hooked up with the other six
girls and headed for the duck pond,
the blushed sky tongued with scarlet licks.
Chris led me away from the rest
to the blue-tinged shelter of high fronds
and when she kissed me soft and long a
host of sparrows glided from the dark crest
of Scrabo over the vale of Kiltonga.

But when we went back things had gone skew-whiff
for Snot had mouthed off that some badly
blown-up bastard or other deserved what he got
and Greener took a God Almighty huff
and launched himself at him, the upshot
of which was a kicking for Greener, Snot
in a thunder, storming off with three
of the girls to grab the hold of a spliff.

Aye half a sore head
Greener said, the other half
thinks it might be dead.
The three girls still with him sniggered.
How can you be happy?
Chris snapped. Don't be such a B-
side, one slurred back, licking her finger
to daub his torn lips' globs of red.

Chris stormed off in a thunder
down a path of hazels and wych elms,
their long shadows. I followed through a blur
of foxglove, columbine, tall ferns,
the trickle of a hidden brook, the whirr
of a far-off helicopter's rotors.
And now I hear the telephone ring
shrill and short the next morning,

the vacuum it brings; but right then
I followed her through dog-walk lanes,
scrub, empty fields and wasted glens
to where lead mines stretched for acres,
where we came across an old knacker
sat bolt upright on a deckchair
by an oil drum in the middle of nowhere
in particular, watching us draw near.

As we walked past in a slow motion haze
he mouthed an undecodable refrain
with hay in his beard and burning eyes,
spitting out his mantra again and again
in a fury of midges and horseflies.
And the discombobulation I felt in his gaze,
out of body and undermined,
was how I'd come to feel most of the time.

She kissed me, then walked off under darkened leaves
and I stood still, watching her leave.
And I wish she wandered broad and far
to that point on the horizon
where sky and sea become one,
where she wrapped the sky around her
like a blue cotton shawl and danced upon the waves.
But she went home to Ballycullen.

I've not been down that way since.
Nothing of those times can be changed
although their connotations constantly change
and I can't pin them down: my words like dust
as if ears of grain gleaned long before
by someone else, leaving only dry husks.
Do what I might, the mind implores
I stand there still, seeking a glimpse

of ribbon-braided hair. I reach out
and clutch at hollows — the telephone
ringing, red eyes, bilious refrains
in the ear, wilted columbine, foxglove,
fallen hazels, the constant spout
of a hidden brook purling through my brain.
And memory is looking on as love
walks off down a darkened green lane.

Green Odes

Get off your arsehole son, the end is nigh.
You got high
on your hellfire, didn't you? Well tired of you
I walked until my feet screamed.
I walked until it seemed
one thing was always reflected in another,
all days interconnected. O mother
with the dong of a bell
in my ear I set out my own stall: if the end is near they can all
go to hell.

❖

I'll write green odes, walking mean roads
with damaged feet, through ravaged wheat
fields drooled with pus, an unwheeled school bus
in a ditch, rabbits and birds
flitched to squirts and gizzards,
broken-hipped deer addled in the dirt,
their blackened lips queer with curdled yoghurt
under a red sky,
the rotten wind a hot pin
in the eye.

Scapegoat

After a botched job
on Cliftonville Road,
someone over-itchy on the trigger,
McCandless, his first job as driver, with a bloke
from another cell he doesn't know,
his anorak still spattered
with blood-smatter and boke,
is to hide on Scrabo Hill in a green
two-man tent that's light as a kite
with a bin bag of corned beef and baked beans —
be thankful for it ye gob-
shite —
until they figure
how to handle the matter.

❖

Ah wis havin a cracker wee dream
lass night — there wis this wet thing
in mah ear. Then ah woke an seen
it wis a rat. At least a mouse.
Jesus, ah'm so cold ah'll go blind.
An ah swear ah'm gettin thin.
An if ah see one more fuckin tin
a cold baked bloody beans.
Could they nat ave bought Heinz?
Could they nat jus hide us in a house
in Ballybeen?
Christ, at this rate, if we wait
any longer it'll be nineteen
hundred and eighty-fuckin-eight.

❖

McCandless adjusts to the night.
He stalks and creeps among high ferns
and purple loosestrife, cuts his shins on gorse,
munches on what he hopes is watercress
and clover, looking down at the town's
red, yellow, blue, white lights and slow cars.
In the sandstone quarry a black-winged
bird glides in circles under the cigar-
ring glows of stars. He etches UFF
on soft rock and risks sounding out
the echo of the quarry, startled,
then dejected by the gulf of darkness
made more empty as the hill calls back to him:
FUCK OFF . . . FUCK OFF . . . OFF . . . OFF . . . FF . . . F . . .

❖

Beneath the hill's turreted tower,
imperial man's fantastical cock,
McCandless looks over lego-
sized bungalows,
demesnes and estates
curved around
the tongue-tip of the lough,
the hard men of the town
burning late
in a rapture
of fear, visions of damnation,
internationalization,
negro cocks,
rods, gag balls, Margaret Thatcher.

❖

Jesus, ye don't talk much,
do ye? We've been here how
long? Must be like forty
days an forty
fuckin nights by now
an next ta nuthin from ye — such
a big Mr Mystery.
Gie us yer share a tha corned dog
would ye? Skinny beardy
bastard. No fuckin odds
ah suppose. Yer too tight.
Christ, ah'm so hungry
ah could ate tha lamb ah god!
Jesus Christ could ye at least gimme a light?

❖

McCandless scrunches along a loose-stone path
under the new moon, then scurries over the spurge
of the path-bank, into a barley field
sloping down to the houses of an estate.
He peers through back windows at new kitchens.
A mousy-haired woman scrapes half-full plates
of potatoes into the bin and sighs
out at what must be her own reflection.
Looking for cracks in the curtains of bedrooms
he hits the jackpot: a young brunette yawns,
arches her back, unbuttons her blouse. He gawks
at the down of her armpits as she bunches
her hair and vanishes. The leash
of her bra strap. The coarse wet barley stalks.

❖

On moonslicked fairways of the golf course
McCandless finds mushrooms. On all fours
he eats like a goat. Soon he's in a bunker
looking at stars. He sees myxomatized
rabbits staring hollow-eyed at nothing.
A Capri screeches across the putting green
with smashed bonnet, bullet holes in the windscreen.
A giant woman with the head of a frog,
the body of Linda Lusardi, peels off flesh-
coloured knickers, croaks in a broad brogue:
Now, you know you want to. He pounces
on a stray black dog in a quarry lane.
He holds it aloft, blood spilling
over him, yelling Who the fuck are ye?

❖

Jesus, they're gonna kill me.
No doubt.
Gonna take me out.
Bury me under a tree
in Killynether.
But wha's bin tha point
ah makin us hang about?
Waitin fer never.
Ah could go an smoke whapper joints
in Florida an sell second-hand
motors. Jesus, wid ye listen tah me?
Ah could go tah fuckin Scotland!
Christ, ah don't know.
Where you gonna go?

❖

Come back to the tent at dawn
McCandless is unsurprised to find
himself alone, with no trace that someone
else has been there at all. All skin and bones
he lies down as mizzling rain fattens
to a downpour, thudding the tent walls,
his breath a brume in the fetid tent air.
With nothing to hit out at there's nothing
there. Surprised that he feels
his skull's been flipped open and he's been
filled to the brim with ashes
he touches his face, all matted beard,
grime, grease and pus, staring into
hollow green darkness. Ack, Jesus!

❖

When they quietly climb the hill
with a gun and two shovels
they find nothing but a pile of barley seeds
on the tent floor. Spread out and look,
one says. Another asks, what for?
If he's smart he's in Scotland.
But they hunt the hill's circle
until they go round the bend
convinced a furtive pair of eyes
looks out from every sycamore,
copse and covert, every clump of tall ferns.
They stop at the edge of Killynether.
On the coarse bark of an ash tree
is etched: *No Surrender*

The Wake

There's a wake on at the McLavertys'
after Bill McLaverty's heart gave out
when for each night and day for the past forty
years the fear was he'd be blown up or shot
in the head like a malevolent goat.

Security my arse. Mercenary
more like, said Dolores Burchill
when he'd last left for Kabul, or Mogadishu.
Now his cronies with thin hair and large
whiskies form well-practised circles.

If they grew back their black bushed sideburns
it'd be like old times, God help us all —
his regalia from the Reserves
still on the wall — just lay down the orange
and brown diamond-patterned carpet in the hall.

What the hell was he up to out there,
an old man? asks someone. Hard bastard
and hooked on it, someone says — knew such tricks
from back thon — making a packet teaching
what it means to police your back yard.

I was in his back yard facing the barley
field with Spud, his son. Ah fuck, here's ma Da,
Spud said. And through golden blowing stalks
Bill marched up with his rifle, red with whiskey.
Spud quipped: out huntin fer the 'RA!

His grandchildren sit hooked on handheld
consoles while his ex-wife frets over ham
sandwiches with a tremor in her hand.
Then photos come out: Bill with sash
and bowler hat, Bill with Lambeg drum,

Bill at his daughter's graduation,
Bill at a peace and reconciliation conference,
Bill at The Robinson Centre gym,
Bill at The Odyssey to see *Brokeback Mountain*,
Bill at the world's largest Titanic visitor experience.

Stand hard, give her respect, but let her know
who's boss, Bill said, lining up gunked paint pots.
Never give the dirty bastards an inch.
Now aim and pull. Ack! Fer fuck's sake!
Years after Spud topped himself with a head shot.

Now the barley field swoons in late twilight.
The town's lights look like harbour lights.
The house is moored in changed lands.
A few old boys try a song, ill at ease,
the wind and windows picking a fight,

waiting for the big man to come home,
for paperwork to be issued,
riding the night skies, over fervid cities,
oil-black oceans, in a trail of thick fumes
bound for Belfast from Kabul, or Mogadishu.

Morning

To wake up is weird.
A clone of yourself,
you don't know where
you went, when you weren't here.
It looks like nowhere.

The night's storm of memories,
hex of dreams, has lifted.
A shower rinses you clean
again — good to go
on to the next night of memories, dreams.

Their interventions.
Moving on is more and more
like trying to reach an invented
somewhere you've already been.
To be there better than before.

You rush to catch your only bus
wishing you could enter the blue
day like a vast meteorological
disturbance. But you do not pass
through life, it passes through you

the way the night passed
through on its way to who
knows where. And, though it looks
as if it had just come around,
that sun was already there.

The Scattering

Gone through the half-hearted window
that gives like a watery eye
onto the East, the blushlight of dawn
on scuzzed rooftops, scrolled hills;

gone over open-mouthed duck ponds,
decked lawns, a populace dreaming
of ordinary sex; gone with limitless texts
through the gridded air's dataflow,

the wheesht of elm leaves in the air,
a rustling blue polyester blouse;
gone with lost souls, their children
photostreams in the cloud,

indebted and encased in metal
and the motion of their cars past yellow
fields, roundabouts, the dead everywhere;
gone into the excitation of particles

and elements in contact with other
elements and particles like peedie
heads in a primary school playground
rushing away from fathers, mothers:

as I turn away, face the room I'm in,
half of me is already out the window
to chase and meet the scattering day
heading West, as if to say, well, hello.

The Sweeping After

Outside the big storm is lifting.
A wreckage of leavings,
blown litter and sludged matter,
puddles of tarnished water,
mess the green. And it's dead
easy to turn over, bury the head,

not bother with the sweeping
when you're closed in,
door bolted against the weather;
although the mussy hutch within,
stale and fusky, also needs
a revolution of fresh air.

A black cat fuffs in the hedge's smeuse
when you pull the curtains, face up
to the light, your brow and heavy eyes
like a seabird, under crystal blue skies,
wading in an oil slick. And in the cup
of your ear a waking baby starts to mewl.

Each newborn mind is a wonder
and a cure for the boo-hoo-hoo
of our own soured sensoriums
would be to inhabit one
by proxy for a minute or two.
So while you wonder

why you should bother to clear the dreck
that wraps its mucor and plastic
over everything, because everything
will die after jiggling with brief meaning
anyhow — clones and drones all that's left —
remember each moment in time's a death

but also a birth. To get to the nub
of the matter, comfort that wee chub,
clammy in your arms, saying bu-bu-bu
as it radiates beatitude through
your solar plexus — you'll wish the words
in which you'll cast that feeling afterwards

were not the ciphers of a hollow code
but suffused with the luminance
of fields in late spring, where you held wheat ears
in your hand and they seemed to glow
and gesture beyond themselves to a candescence
pulsing behind the surface of things,

although we can't advance through the mirror.
We are like a blue kingfisher
perched on a moss green branch that's cleft
over a rowan-lined river
staring into its wonked self-
reflection upon burnished water.

It awaits the clearing of darkness
to see within, catch its prey.
Without the dark, light would be tyrannous.
Without night, no looking forward to the day.
Exchange subject and object at will.
The chaos of leavings still gathers and swills

and it's time for a clearing. By brightness
blinded, we must sweep through,
knowing nothing advances
but what is left alive — in memory,
in the mind and in mindlessness —
is called love. Love is constancy

changing, palpable and ungraspable
within the night and day's confusion,
the sweepings of the past,
spinning as the future was when it came
to trade us easy devices for grain,
horses, rope, shipbuilding, ploughs and linen.

River Mouth

If some regions of the brain are foreign
to others, as they say, this might explain
why my moods swing like hips in a hula dance:
now grumped, now chipper, now the essence
of cement, now a gushed river flow.
A woodland river. Green, brown and yellow
limn its banks: sprunt pines and bending sycamores,
song thrushes. It rushes for the shore
the way that urge surged through me, out of my mouth
in sounds not half my own, when I burst forth
into song this morning in the kitchen.
There was no reason to sing. No one to listen.
Happiness comes on like a once-loved song
on the radio — played over in the mind once it's gone.
Useless to follow. It doesn't end, doesn't start:
a river that twists and turns into the unsatnaved heart
of the woods which shift in their shade perpetually,
sunlight pooling in the heads of the trees
while a congregation of sound fills the air,
pulls the ear. Useless to ponder where
that happiness went to, where it had been:
I can't even catch the dark-yellow-light-brown-flecked green
while I follow the many-voiced river through downs
and drumlins, train stations at the border of town,
past warehouses, vast retail lots, car-stained
miles of suburban families detained
in dream homes. To apprehend such density
of life would be to hold fresh to memory
each page of each book on a full forty-foot shelf.
The mind can't keep up with itself
and I get lost in town — masonry changed by whims
of weather, helter-skelter buildings on thin
streets huddled together: granite and whinstone,
polished ashlar, red sandstone, blonde and brown stone,
many-sized windows numerous as rain-

drops in the air, each an eye cast on this drained
world, each an eye giving onto an inner
realm I peer into, staring at the décor
of strange rooms, going 'ooohh', 'yuk', or 'hmm?',
catching a glimpse of a grey cluttered room:
a woman at a desk, rubbing her aching neck,
her tired eyes, turning away from her book,
laptop, stacked plates and cups, scribbled words,
turning away from this tasked world towards
an inner realm: her thoughts like quicksilver shoals
in motion through a green water-blue soul,
her eye a twilight moon over this wood's
gushing river that I follow under the mood
swings of sycamores, fearful of the pines,
wondering where on earth does the time
go while the weather turns and cold winds
ruffle the witch hazel, rustle the whin,
wilting sweet gum. Smokebush withers.
Woodland thins. Crows caw and circle
the blush sky, mild above autumn's
mown fields, borderlands, foreign regions
where the river, many rivers, empty
into a dark sea, the mind of nobody
where whatever it was that was borne in song
floats and dims on the brim of meaning.

One Summer Morning

in memory of Raymond Potter

When you left
the house, where many were your guest,
on your last morning
I hope you stopped
on top of your steep steps
to take it in,
the bright field on the slopes
of the hill and the blue lift over the rooftops.

It isn't the ground we yield
that has us run away wild
through green fields
nor crows that sweep through the turned
sky over rivers as the crust
of the sun rusts on mild
estates and suburbs at dusk.
But how their image will burn.

Though nothing remains, still
that morning is where we might seek you.
A breeze blows in off the lough's blue.
A house sparrow flies into the cloud
as if on a mission.
Up steep steps, the slope of the shining hill,
would we find a note on the door:
Gone fishing!

The Rose Beds

Late afternoon in Lady Dixon Park,
dank in the February cold,
blocks of flowerbeds
without flowers jut from the grass banks,

straight-edged pits coloured sleechy aubergine,
rows upon rows of them in regimental
rectangles, runes casting a hold
over the rigid air and kempt green.

Dour as used ashtrays,
from a height the lawn must look
like a barcode. The surrounding city
is dead fish and mushroom grey.

Dismal slabs, large open graves
lacking the finality
of being filled, like mouths to feed:
the flowerbeds impose their geometry.

Even the sky seems a grid,
planned and patterned but out of place
above curving pathways lined with birches,
the spick-and-span hedgerows' sculpted arches,

the bramble of a copse, wiry-thin,
brittle as bones behind skin.
The flowerbeds bring to mind a prison,
how the mind is a prism

of formulaic dreams, arcane rules,
obscure integers, dormant machines,
the grist of order, maths at High School.
Then the wintercold scene becomes the green

portacabin of a classroom
with taupe interior, Ms Bacon
intoning equations, the boredom aching,
desks gridded in blocks of doom,

rows upon rows of calculations undone.
And I am drawn to nothing, a moth to the light,
but your bottle green skirt and laddered cream tights,
drifting, dreaming of a time when we will come

together at long last,
late afternoon in Lady Dixon Park,
arm in arm to see a Mardi Gras
of roses bamboozle the grass banks.

The curved city beyond fizzes and pops
as we walk past lemonade yellow Lemon Drops,
lavender Blue Girls, mauve Shocking Blues,
yellow, peach and deep orange Voodoos.

Shading our path, birch leaves droop
over yellow ivory edged in red Betty Boops,
cool orange Tropicanas,
cotton candy pink Rose de Alhambras.

Past violet red with white eye Space Odysseys,
deep yellow-red blend Celebrities,
I follow you to salmon blushing pink Hold Me Tights,
cream flushing scarlet Double Delights.

From the lip of your jeans peeks a turquoise thong
as you saunter by redder than red Cardinal Songs,
pure white Sugar Moons, orange-juice orange Vavooms,
cream blushing to strawberry coral Brigadoons.

You smirk like Lolita past buttermilk Perditas,
flush pink Dream Weavers, dark red Night Fevers.
And as we lie, reeking with nectar,
beside shimmering silvery pink Sweet Surrenders,

I am all fingers and thumbs,
stumped by lavender blushing purple Fragrant Plums.
You say 'you win some, you lose some',
plucking a deep magenta Winsome.

Then a rule-stick whacks the desk.
The classroom vibrates. The seething zits
of Ms Bacon's eyes look possessed.
I blink. And see blurred lamps have been lit.

Dusk is sulking through Lady Dixon Park,
by the hedgerows, across the scumped
grass banks. Freezing winds rasp the bark-
bare birches, hardening these sullen humps

of flowerbeds. A flotilla in the fog,
a curl of lights, the city in the distance
floats — below the surface its cogs
churning on in a rage of conveyance.

Like it or lump it,
this is where we are: allotted
our place on a well-worn circuit.
Knowing they have been plotted,

will the roses be engulfed in the blaze
of themselves, consumed in their spark,
or just preen and glaze
within their own quotation marks?

Perhaps all pattern is a plan to die
reasonably, all things apportioned a role:
birds will fall from the sky,
words will be hollowed back into holes

like these rows upon rows of open
mouths in the earth, swallowing down,
rooting for a rhythm,
turning nouns to verbs, catching sounds,

wanton colours, new reasons
to keep going, waiting for the season
to come around, when such blank mounds
will lift the light of roses from the ground.

Night Song for Rosie

Look up at the night's wide dome
adrift through the calm of your mind,
an open vat of deep silent wine —

like floating on the lakes of the moon —
reflecting stars, a looking glass of dreams,
your eyes, upon noiseless waters.

These waters will evaporate and rise,
stew and frown into stormy weather
to murk the stars, darken your eyes.

This will come. This will go. Rest your mind,
pressing down, light unto a screen.
Don't let yourself be tormented.

The stars are grapes swelling on a vine,
aching to fall, to be fermented
in the Lake of Softness, Lake of Time.

The Sweeping

When you're cobwebbed,
    your head's stale bread,
batteries low as can go;
    when all you might say
slubs your mouth and dulls to clay:

get yourself outdoors
        when the weather turns mean.
  I mean
when gravid howl-soon scum clouds,
        big bad bruised bastards,
fat soiled swollen arses plunged
        down the scuzzed bowl of the sky
gather and gulder in hordes
    like thugs-for-hire far too keen on their jobs,
as if there was terror in heaven,
        as if a dark angel might render
        a cumulonimbus-shaped
megaphone to dictate a contract of surrender:
          'Abide by our terms and you will learn
    of the ecstasy that burned in Job
  as he shaved his head, threw himself
upon the ground and worshipped.'

Get yourself outside to suck
        up the calamity
of hound-black howlers
huffed up over the frazzled nerve-
        ends of needle-furze,
thrawn wheat, barley, maize, bulrush,
        over the motion-sick
surface of fast-frumpled reservoirs,
    discomfuffled lakes,
frothing loughs, scampering rivers
    that will soon break

    their banks, scuttled poons,
          elms and larches convulsing in the air
          like headbangers' hair
in the throes of death
         metal music.

Get yourself flubbed and freaked
          by screamers that fly at
    your senses, sidewinders in a riot
of knuckle-dustered
        blow-you-four-ways
superfuzzed nutter-gusters,
          and prepare to get nailed
     as the sky rips
its strained skin to begin
        its bellyache,
bowel-shift and waterbreak,
    a hissed dissle
       growing into
       a trillion-splattered sizzle
         growing into
         a zillion form-seeking missiles
of water a minute
        launched in a bungalow-
          battering crescendo
of hard clots and ingots of hail
        that the dust, dirt, mire
   and loan gollop
until the ground parts
      as if with parting
legs to fart loose dirt-dregs,
        a glair and squelch,
        ooze and dreel
of curdled quags
      gubbled and squinnied

   in hinnying gallops
              of pelleted rain,
     flinty sleet-splatters that mawl
and serrate the sculpted
suburban hedges,
      smash the manicured lawn-
grass, gnash the lady's smock,
            slash the foxfire,
    thrash junipers and elders
in a scatter of sprays,
    sprigs and tatters.

Let rain scrub the scroofy walls
            of banks, bookies, bars,
    detached houses,
corner shops,
    their soot-scunged windows;
let rain dance stocious on rooftops;
      let rain riddle and ding
the bonnets of sprootzy-dootzy cars,
            now scrunted and stricken;
    let rain sluice and juice spew-
pools of coagulated chicken
            nuggets, vodka jellies,
      overspilling belly-busted
back-alley bin-bilge,
      heaving nidorous hunks
   of over-thwunked milge;
let rain scutter and whang
    the scudded cronk
            and slag of industrial yards;
      let rain water-cannon
goose shit, lucerne,
      scumber from farmyards

and swish and swill in potato
    drills;
let rain slish down on silage,
        bones and ammonia;
    let rain scour clean the vents
and sills of haggard hills,
        the land you stand on,
the greywacke, siltstone,
        saltmarsh,
    the seizure of the shore.

And when you look up to see
        gashed light through the thunder-
    head feeling
gingerish in thaw-rain,
        skin-raw, dirled and dinted,
flenched, pogo-brained, infinitesimal,
        flushed out
in thrall to the after-din
        and after-fall,
you can come back inside,
    flurred and flummoxed but unbleared,
        rinsed to the hollows,
    uprooted and reeling
    yet circumfluent.
Good to go.

Acknowledgements

Grateful acknowledgement is made to the following publications in which some of these poems, or versions of them, originally appeared: *The Cincinnati Review, The Evergreen: A Season in the North, Irish Pages, The Istanbul Review, The Manchester Review, Peter Fallon: Poet, Publisher, Editor and Translator,* ed. Richard Rankin Russell (Irish Academic Press, 2013), *Poetry International, Poetry London, Poetry Review,* and *The Yellow Nib.*